Agile Software Development

Agile Software Development is an introduction to agile software development methods. Agile methods try to diminish complexity, increase transparency, and reach a deployable product in a shorter time frame. Agile methods use an iterative and incremental approach to minimize risks and to avoid maldevelopment. The book gives a short introduction to agile methods and agile software development principles. It serves as a study book and as a reference manual. Based on the official Scrum Guide, the book also covers other topics such as best practices for agile software development and agile testing. It targets practitioners who want to start with agile software development, as well as developers or project managers who already use agile methodologies. The book can be read from the beginning, but each chapter has been written in a way so it can be read individually.

Peter Wlodarczak is an IT consultant in Data Analytics and Machine Learning. Born in Basel, Switzerland, he holds a Master's degree and a PhD from the University of Southern Queensland, Australia. He has many years of experience in large software engineering and data analysis projects. He has published more than 20 papers and book chapters in this area and has presented his work in many conferences. His research interests include, among others, Machine Learning, eHealth, and Bio Computing.

T0353594

IT Pro Practice Notes

Practical Guide to IT Problem Management
By Andrew Dixon
2022

Cybertax: Managing the Risks and Results
By George K. Tsantes, James Ransome
2023

Agile Software Development
By Peter Wlodarczak
2024

Agile Software Development

Peter Wlodarczak

CRC Press
Taylor & Francis Group
Boca Raton London New York

CRC Press is an imprint of the
Taylor & Francis Group, an **informa** business
AN AUERBACH BOOK

First edition published 2024
by CRC Press
2385 NW Executive Center Drive, Suite 320, Boca Raton FL 33431

and by CRC Press
4 Park Square, Milton Park, Abingdon, Oxon, OX14 4RN

CRC Press is an imprint of Taylor & Francis Group, LLC

ISBN: 978-1-032-29465-0 (hbk)
ISBN: 978-1-032-29464-3 (pbk)
ISBN: 978-1-003-30170-7 (ebk)

DOI: 10.1201/9781003301707

Typeset in Nimbus font
by KnowledgeWorks Global Ltd.

Contents

List of Figures

List of Tables

Chapter 1

Introduction

This script is an introduction into agile software development methods. In software engineering, a method defines a structured, goal-driven approach to reach a meaningful result. A method describes formalized procedures that have proven to be useful and expedient.

Classical models such as the waterfall model or the V-model follow a sequential approach. They divide the development process into phases, which are passed through linearly. A new phase is only started if the previous phase has been completed. In practice, classic models have often shown to be sluggish and inflexible. Because of these limitations, agile methods have gained in popularity over the past decades. Agile methods try to diminish complexity, increase transparency, and reach a deployable product in a shorter time frame. Agile methods use an iterative and incremental approach to minimize risks and to avoid maldevelopment.

DOI: 10.1201/9781003301707-1

This script gives a short introduction into agile methods and agile software development principles. It serves as study book and as a reference manual. It is based on the official Scrum Guide [1] but it also covers other topics such as best practices for agile software development and agile testing. It targets practitioners who want to start with agile software development as well as developers or project managers who already use agile methodologies.

The book can be read from the beginning, but each chapter has been written in a way so it can be read individually.

Chapter 2

Classical Models

2.1 Waterfall Model

The waterfall model is a linear model, where the development process is divided into phases. The phases are processed sequentially. A new phase is only started if the previous one has been completed.

The phases can vary depending on the project and the approaches used; typical phases are shown in figure 2.1. Usually a project starts with requirements analysis to understand the needs and goals of the customer, but sometimes phases such as conception or initiation are also used.

The requirements phase captures the demands in a requirements document. During the design phase, the software architecture is elaborated. In the implementation phase, the software is programmed and integrated. Testing is the systematic discovery of bugs and defects. Testing is often broken down into different types such as integration testing and user acceptance testing. Testing is covered in more detail in

DOI: 10.1201/9781003301707-2

3

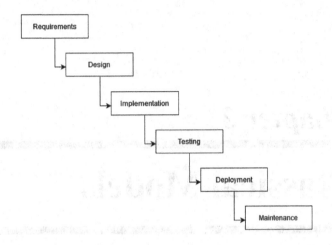

Figure 2.1: Waterfall model.

Chapter 6. During the deployment, the software is installed and integrated with other systems such as backend systems and databases. Finally, in the maintenance phase, the final product goes into production.

The phases are often represented as cascade where the flow passes in one direction downward, hence the name waterfall model. Waterfall models have sometimes been criticized for its rigidity and lack of flexibility.

2.2   V-Model

The V-model is an extension of the waterfall model. It also breaks down the development process into phases. But after the implementation phase, the phases are bent upward giving it the V shape where the name comes from as shown in figure 2.2. The goal of the V-model is to have full test coverage in

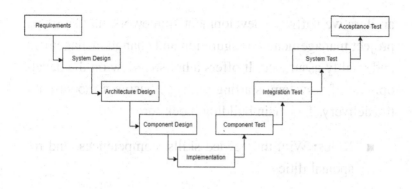

Figure 2.2: V-model.

every phase. The V-model shows the relationship between each phase and its corresponding test phase.

As with the waterfall model, the phases can vary depending on the literature and the project's needs, but, except for the implementation phase, every phase has a corresponding test phase where the product is validated for its correctness and completeness.

The V-model has been critizised not only for its inflexibility and rigidness but also for giving managers a false sense of security. Since the tests scripts are written in advance, often critical parts are not tested since they have been overlooked during test design. The V-model has also no inherent ability to respond to change.

2.3 RUP

The Rational Unified Process (RUP) was introduced at the end of the 1990s. RUP has addressed many of the shortcomings of sequential processes such as the rigidity and inflexibility in the waterfall model and the V-model. It is an iterative software development framework that supports project management, configuration and change management and quality assurance. It offers a holistic view on the development of a system, starting with the business model until the delivery. The main building blocks are:

- **Roles:** With the needed skills, competences, and responsibilities

- **Work products:** Describing the result of a task including the product, the model, and documentation produced

- **Tasks:** Describing the work unit assigned to a role

RUP is not a single prescriptive approach to software development but rather an adaptable framework where parts can be used or omitted as required by the project. It provides many artifacts and descriptions for many activities in a project. RUP is based on the Unified Process and can be tailored to meet the development project's needs. It is a commercial framework, and a test can be taken to become a certified RUP specialist.

Chapter 3

Agile Methods

Agile Methods address two basic issues in software development:

- The high speed at which software is developed today

- The insight that changes to the original requirements are the rule, not the exception

In agile software development, the whole project is divided into small steps. At the end of each, step there is an added value for the customer. In iterations of a few weeks, called sprints, the customer receives a working and internally tested software increment.

Originally developed for software engineering, agile methods are widely used today for other types of projects.

DOI: 10.1201/9781003301707-3

3.1 The Agile Manifest

Agile software development became popular in 1990. Agile development was a response to the sluggish development processes and the sequential approach that strictly followed the functional specification. These methods have the big disadvantage that the original requirements are often obsolete during the development phase or new requirements come up which weren't known at the beginning of the project.

In February 2001, Kent Beck and other representatives of agile software development formulated their core values in the agile manifesto [2]. The agile manifesto defines a set of values and principles derived from a broad range of software development frameworks. The four guiding principles of the agile manifesto are:

- **Individuals and interactions** over processes and tools

- **Working software** over comprehensive documentation

- **Customer collaboration** over contract negotiation

- **Responding to change** over following a plan [2]

While the values on the right are important, the values on the left (in bold) are weighted higher by the signatories. Among the 17 initial signatories of the manifesto are also the founders of Extreme programming (XP) and Scrum.

3.1.1 Agile principles

The agile manifesto lists 12 principles:

■ Our highest priority is to satisfy the customer through early and continuous delivery of valuable software.

■ Welcome changing requirements, even late in development. Agile processes harness change for the customer's competitive advantage.

■ Deliver working software frequently, from a couple of weeks to a couple of months, with a preference to the shorter timescale.

■ Business people and developers must work together daily throughout the project.

■ Build projects around motivated individuals. Give them the environment and support they need, and trust them to get the job done.

■ The most efficient and effective method of conveying information to and within a development team is face-to-face conversation.

■ Working software is the primary measure of progress.

■ Agile processes promote sustainable development. The sponsors, developers, and users should be able to maintain a constant pace indefinitely.

■ Continuous attention to technical excellence and good design enhances agility.

■ Simplicity – the art of maximizing the amount of work not done – is essential.

■ The best architectures, requirements, and designs emerge from self-organizing teams.

■ At regular intervals, the team reflects on how to become more effective, then tunes and adjusts its behavior accordingly [3]

Although the agile manifesto provides a good basis, it is not very helpful in terms of concrete, practical instructions for action. Moreover, the principles can be interpreted in different ways. This is why different agile methods have emerged.

3.2 Extreme programming

XP is an agile software development methodology that aims to improve software quality and addresses responsiveness to changing customer requirements through short development cycles and frequent releases. It also advocates pair programming, full unit test coverage of the code, code reviews, and flat hierarchies. Contrary to other methodologies such as Scrum, XP can be adopted by one developer whereas Scrum requires a team.

XP is based on five values and a set of rules. The five values are **simplicity**, **communication**, **feedback**, **respect**, and **courage** [5]. They state that simple solutions are preferable over complex ones (Occam's razor), not only in technical but also in organizational terms, and that communication and feedback are essential for the success of a team. But that care must be taken to treat each other with respect, while at the same time demonstrating courage, for example, in addressing unpleasant issues.

XP covers the entire cycle from project planning to testing. Many rules of XP have become a matter of course today,

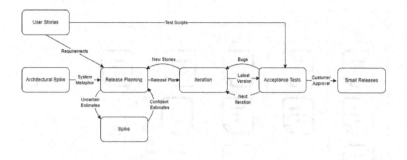

Figure 3.1: Extreme programming.

for example, an iterative approach, the use of user stories and proof-of-concepts, and the consistent application of coding guidelines and unit tests. However, in XP, the organizational level is almost completely missing.

XP uses spike solutions to explore potential solutions. A spike solution is a very simple program to address a specific problem ignoring the rest of the solutions. They are rarely good enough to be used in the solution. Spikes are used to reduce risk and to improve the quality of the effort estimate of a user story.

XP being an agile methodology is all about embracing change. Instead of an upfront design of the entire solution, it creates iterative designs, planning is done before each iteration, and testing happens as soon as possible. A development cycle is typically short, usually just a week. The whole cycle of an XP project is shown in figure 3.1.

3.3 Kanban

Kanban is a lean method for organizing work across human systems. The basic idea of Kanban is that of a common

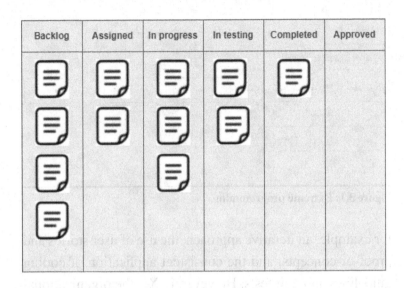

Backlog	Assigned	In progress	In testing	Completed	Approved

Figure 3.2: Kanban board.

Kanban board, which is divided into several columns, sometimes called swim lanes as shown in figure 3.2. For example, there might be a column for the tasks still to be completed, a column for the tasks currently in progress, a column for the tasks to be tested, and a column for the tasks already completed. The individual tasks, in turn, are noted on cards that are gradually moved from left to right on the board depending on the progress.

The special thing about Kanban is that these columns are limited in their capacity. This means, for example, that only a limited amount of cards may be placed in the column for the tasks to be tested. This makes sense because, even in reality, only limited test capacities are available, which is also reflected on the Kanban board along the way.

The goal of Kanban is to be able to identify bottlenecks and delays in a timely manner and, ideally, to resolve them in order to enable the most even and steady flow of cards possible without the process coming to a standstill. So unlike Scrum, Kanban does not rely on recurring iterations, but rather on a continuous flow. Kanban boards are usually used in Scrum and other methodologies for planning iterations and releases and for managing team capacity.

There are other methods, such as Behaviour-Driven Development (BDD) or Continuous Flow, but this book will cover Scrum, the most widely used agile method today. Kanban is often used in Scrum as Scrum board.

Chapter 4

Scrum

4.1 Introduction to Scrum

Scrum is an iterative methodology for developing and delivering products in a complex environment. Originating in software development, it has been applied to projects in many fields including research, marketing, and frontier technology. Scrum forms an organizational framework that provides rules for teamwork but says nothing about how the work is actually to be done.

Scrum is:

- Iterative and incremental

- Lightweight

- Easy to understand

- Transparent

DOI: 10.1201/9781003301707-4

The Scrum frameworks consists of teams with their associated roles, artifacts and events. Scrum divides the whole development cycle into small iterations called sprints, where each sprint is about two to four weeks long. Scrum is easy to understand but difficult to master.

4.2   Scrum Team

The Scrum team delivers products iteratively and incrementally. It consists of three to nine members and is self-organizing. It decides how to best accomplish their work without being dictated from outside. It has all the competences needed to accomplish their work.

The Scrum team consists of three roles:

■ **Product Owner (PO)**: Interfaces with customers and manages requirements and their prioritization

■ **Development Team (Dev Team)**: Implements the requirements

■ **Scrum Master (SM)**: Responsible for the correct implementation of Scrum and empowers the Scrum team

4.2.1   Product Owner

The PO is responsible for maximizing the value of the product that results from the work of the Scrum team. How this is done can vary greatly depending on the organization, the Scrum team, and individual.

The PO is also responsible for effectively managing the PB, which includes:

■ Developing and explicitly communicating the product goal

■ Creating and clearly communicating product backlog items

■ Arranging PB elements

■ Ensuring that the PB is transparent, visible, and understood

The PO may perform the above work or delegate responsibility to others. Regardless, the PO remains accountable.

For the PO to be successful, the entire organization must respect his decisions. These decisions are visible in the content and sequence of the PB and through the inspectable increment at sprint review.

The PO is a person, not a committee. The PO can represent the needs of many stakeholders in the PB. Those who want to change the PB can do so by trying to convince the PO.

4.2.2 Scrum Master

The SM is responsible for establishing Scrum as defined in the Scrum Guide [1]. He does this by helping everyone understand Scrum theory and practice, both within the Scrum team and the organization.

The SM is responsible for the effectiveness of the Scrum team. He does this by empowering the Scrum team to improve its practices within the Scrum framework.

SMs are true leaders who serve the Scrum team and the larger organization.

The SM serves the Scrum team in several ways, including:

■ Coaching team members in self-management and cross-functionality;

■ Supporting the Scrum team in focusing on creating high-quality increments that meet the Definition of Done (DoD);

■ Removing impediments to the Scrum team's progress; and

■ Ensuring that all Scrum events occur and are positive, productive, and kept within the time box.

The SM serves the PO in several ways, including:

■ Helping identify techniques for effective product goal definition and PB management;

■ Helping the Scrum team understand the need to create clear and concise PB elements;

■ Helping establish empirical product planning for a complex environment; and

■ Facilitate collaboration with stakeholders when desired or needed.

The SM serves the organization in several ways, including:

- Leading, training, and coaching the organization in the implementation of Scrum;

- Planning and advising on Scrum implementations within the organization;

- Helping staff and stakeholders understand and implement an empirical approach to complex work; and

- Removing barriers between stakeholders and Scrum teams.

4.2.3 Dev Team

The Dev Team, the developers, are the people on the Scrum team who are involved in creating any aspect of a usable increment in each sprint. The specific skills required of the developers are often broad, T-shaped skills, and vary with the scope of work. However, the Dev Team is always responsible for:

- Creating a plan for the sprint, the sprint backlog;

- Ensuring quality by adhering to a DoD;

- Adjusting your plan each day toward the sprint goal; and,

- Consulting each other as subject matter experts.

The Dev Team includes approximately three to ten people, and these include all the roles required to implement the project. Thus, a team consists not only of developers but also includes people with other skills and knowledge, for instance database admins and network or security specialists.

4.3 Product Backlog

The starting point for working with Scrum is the so-called PB, which contains the technical requirements in the form of so-called user stories. A user story is a short description of the feature to be developed or the bug to be fixed, but it contains not only the description itself but often also information about the business value that the implementation of this story delivers. The aim is to ensure that stories are not an end in themselves, but always serve a higher goal.

4.3.1 *Product Goal*

The product goal provides context to the PB. It can be thought of as the "why" we are doing all this work. It can be used as the elevator pitch to "What is the Scrum team working on?" The word "goal" is intentional because it describes two things:

■ It's something to strive for.

■ It's measurable when you've achieved it.

The Scrum Guide does not prescribe what the details of a product goal are, allowing Scrum teams to frame the goal in the right way for their context. For example, some Scrum teams work on a quarterly product goal that is very focused, whereas another Scrum team may have a product goal that is very ambitious and high level. Context is everything when setting the product goal.

4.4 User Story

User stories are a technique for describing requirements from a user's perspective using everyday language. In Scrum, user stories are used to formulate the PB entries. A user story describes what product feature the user wants, why he or she wants it, and what it is intended to accomplish.

The form given in figure 4.1 is usually used for user stories.

It is the task of the PO and the team to clarify in the PB Refinement what exactly is meant in a specific user story and what the acceptance criteria should be. In addition, the Dev Team must clarify with the PO whether this user story can be completed at all in one sprint, or whether it must be broken down into smaller stories. All changes and additions as well as other information are also recorded in the PB.

A story that is too large and covers many functions superficially is also called an Epic. It is broken down into more detailed user stories.

The technical implementation is not part of the user story. It is defined during sprint planning. The effort estimation is

Title:	Priority:	Estimate:
User Story: As a [description of user]: I want [functionality]: So that [benefit]:		
Acceptance criteria:		

Figure 4.1: User story.

also done during sprint planning and noted on the user story. Often Kanban boards are used to create and manage user stories.

4.5 Scrum Events

Each event in Scrum is a formal opportunity to review and adjust Scrum artifacts. These events are specifically designed to provide the required visibility. If an event is not performed as prescribed, an opportunity for review and adjustment is lost. Events are used in Scrum to create regularity and minimize the need for meetings not defined in Scrum.

Optimally, all events occur at the same time and place to reduce complexity.

4.5.1 Sprint

In Scrum, the sprint backlog is processed iteratively in so-called sprints, which usually represent periods of two to four weeks, although shorter sprints are preferable. The sprint is a container for all other events. Sprints are the pulse of Scrum, where ideas are turned into business value.

A new sprint starts immediately after the previous sprint is completed. All work required to achieve the product goal, including sprint planning, Daily Scrums, sprint review, and sprint retrospective, takes place within sprints.

At the beginning of a sprint, the team decides which stories should be addressed in joint coordination with the PO. During the sprint, the team meets daily for a meeting, the Daily Scrum, to discuss the current progress and any obstacles or problems that have arisen. The Daily Scrum Meeting is a stand-up meeting and lasts a maximum of 15 minutes.

At the end of each sprint, there is first a review, in which the team presents the successfully implemented stories, which also serves as a technical approval; and then a retrospective, in which the work is discussed at the meta level: What went well? What went badly? What should be kept, changed, or discarded about the way we work together? The team also measures the speed at which it has progressed in order to gradually develop a better baseline for reliable estimates on this basis. This speed, called velocity in Scrum, is often based on point values rather than actual units of time, to deliberately talk about story complexity rather than time.

During the sprint:

■ No changes are made that would jeopardize the sprint goal,

■ The quality standard is not reduced,

■ The PB is refined as needed, and

■ Scope can be clarified and renegotiated with the PO as more becomes known.

A sprint can be considered as a mini-project. Just like in a project, the sprint aims to achieve a specific holistic goal. Each sprint has a defined scope of work, a design, and a flexible plan of what implementation, work, and outcome will lead in the right direction.

If a sprint duration of more than four weeks is chosen, the definition of the result can become more difficult, the complexity increases, and the risk of failure increases. The larger the time horizon, the less predictable it is. Sprints enable predictability by allowing review and adjustments of progress toward a specific sprint goal at least once every four weeks. Sprints also reduce risk to a month's cost. Sprints that are too short increase excessive recurring effort (overhead). A sprint and its phases are shown in figure 4.2.

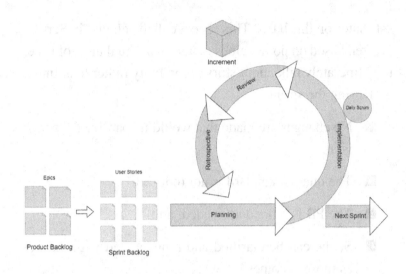

Figure 4.2: Scrum framework.

4.5.2 Sprint Planning

In sprint planning, the work for the upcoming sprint is planned. This plan is created through the collaborative work of the entire Scrum team.

For each week of a sprint, two hours should be used as a time box. The PO ensures that planning takes place and that the participants understand its purpose. He enables the team to successfully complete the planning within the time box.

The PO ensures that the participants are prepared to discuss the key PB elements and how they map to the product goal. The Scrum team may also invite others to participate in sprint planning to provide advice.

Sprint planning should answer two questions:

■ What can be achieved (goal and product increment definition)?

■ How will it be achieved?

It is recommended to answer these two questions separately.

4.5.2.1 Sprint Planning 1: What can be reached?

The entire Scrum team works together to develop an understanding of the work content of the sprint. This includes goal definition for the sprint, as well as the selection of PB entries, which — if they are completed in this sprint — ensure goal achievement. The selection of PB entries moves into the sprint backlog.

The following serve as the starting point for planning:

■ Personnel capacity (attendance time, especially of the Dev Team members) for the quantity

■ Average performance of the Dev Team to date

■ PB for the functionality

Only the Dev Team decides on the quantity of PB entries for the upcoming sprint. Only the team itself can judge what is feasible in the upcoming sprint.

After choosing the PB entries for the sprint (by the Dev Team), the whole Scrum team formulates a sprint goal. The sprint goal forms the benchmark for accomplishing this sprint. It guides the Dev Team in why they are creating this product increment.

4.5.2.2 Sprint Planning 2: How can it be reached?

After the goal is defined and the PB items to be completed are selected for the sprint, the Dev Team decides how it wants to create the product increment so that the functionality is considered "Done" overall.

The Dev Team begins the system design and work necessary to create the functional product increment. The work may vary in size and estimated effort. In any case, the Dev Team should plan enough to forecast what can be completed in the upcoming sprint. The work planned for the first sprint days is broken down into smaller units at the end of planning, which often take less than one day to complete. The Dev Team organizes itself in the implementation of how it approaches the work in the sprint backlog, starting with sprint planning and as needed in the sprint itself.

If the Dev Team finds out during planning that they have taken on too much or too little work, they can renegotiate with the PO on the PB items chosen.

At the end of sprint planning, the Dev Team should be able to describe to the PO and SM how they would like to work as a self-organized team to achieve the sprint goal and create the desired product increment.

Sprint planning is designed to be a maximum of eight hours for a one-month sprint. For shorter sprints, the event is usually shorter.

4.5.2.3   Sprint Goal

If the selected PB items form a functional unit, the goal is easy to define. The sprint goal, the PB items selected for the sprint, and the plan for their delivery are collectively referred to as the sprint backlog. If the sprint backlog is not so homogeneous, the sprint goal can be any unifying element that motivates the Dev Team to work together. For example, the PB entry with the most distinctive functionality as the final product.

In its work, the Dev Team keeps its sprint goal in mind. To achieve it, it implements the appropriate functionality and technology. If it becomes apparent that the scope of work deviates from the original expectations, the Dev Team negotiates a change to the sprint backlog scope for the current sprint together with the PO. This may also involve redefining the goal.

An experienced Dev Team rarely needs to renegotiate during a sprint.

4.5.2.4   Daily Scrum

The Daily Scrum — or Stand-up Meeting — is a time box of 15 minutes, regardless of sprint duration, within which the Dev Team synchronizes its activities and works on planning for the next 24 hours. This is done by reviewing the work since the last Daily Scrum and forecasting the work deliverables that could be achieved by the next Daily Scrum. It should take place at the same time each day in the same place, typically the team's Scrum board.

The following questions should be answered:

■ What have I accomplished since yesterday that will help the Dev Team achieve the sprint goal?

■ What will I accomplish today to help the Dev Team achieve the sprint goal?

■ What obstacles (impediments) do I see that are keeping me or the Dev Team from achieving the sprint goal?

Discussions should be avoided here. Only one person speaks. Only comprehension questions should be asked by listening Dev Team members if absolutely necessary.

The Daily Scrum increases the likelihood that the Dev Team will achieve its sprint goal because it reviews its progress toward the sprint goal and the trend in working through the sprint backlog. The Dev Team should have a day-by-day view of how they want to work together as a self-organized team to achieve the sprint goal and deliver the expected increment at sprint end. Immediately following the Daily Scrum, individual members or the entire Dev Team often meet for more detailed discussions, adjustments, agreements, or rescheduling of work in the sprint.

If the Dev Team is also responsible for conducting the Daily Scrum, the SM teaches the Dev Team how to adhere to the time box and ensures that only Dev Team members actively participate.

Daily Scrums improve communication, eliminate the need for other meetings, identify obstacles to be removed, focus as well as promote rapid decision making, and increase the knowledge level of the Dev Team. The Daily Scrum is a critical meeting for review and adjustment.

4.5.2.5 Sprint Review

At the end of a sprint, a sprint review is carried out to check the product increment created and to adjust the PB if necessary. Together with the Scrum team, the stakeholders also deal with the results of the sprint. Together with any changes to the PB during the sprint, these provide the basis for joint work on possible new items that increase the value of the product. Sprint review is an informal event, not a status report. The increment demonstration is intended as a stimulus for feedback and the basis for collaboration.

One hour per sprint week should be scheduled as a time box. The SM takes care of organizing the event and preparing the participants. He shows all participants how to keep the time box.

The sprint review includes the following elements:

■ The participants are the Scrum team and key stakeholders invited by the PO.

■ The PO explains which PB items are "Done" and which are not.

■ The Dev Team presents what went well during the sprint, and what issues arose, and how they were resolved (if already done).

- The Dev Team demonstrates the "Done" work/ functionality and answers questions about it.

- The PO presents the current status of the PB and provides an updated forecast of the completion date based on progress, if needed.

- All participants work together on what needs to be done next, making the sprint

- An assessment is made of whether new insights into the most valuable next steps have emerged as a result of the market situation or the possible product deployment

- Then, the schedule, budget, potential features, and market expectations for the next expected product release are reviewed.

The result of the sprint review is a revised PB that contains the potential PB entries for the upcoming sprint.

4.5.2.6 Sprint Retrospective

The sprint retrospective is an opportunity for the Scrum team to review itself and create an improvement plan for the upcoming sprint.

It takes place between the sprint review and the next sprint planning. For four-week sprints, a time box of three hours is set. For shorter sprints, it is usually shorter. The SM ensures that the retrospective takes place and that all participants understand its purpose. He ensures that the time box is adhered to and participates as an equal member.

The purpose of the retrospective is to:

■ Review how the past sprint went in terms of the people, relationships, processes, and tools involved

■ Identify the key elements that went well and possible improvements

■ Create a plan for implementing improvements to the way the Scrum team works

The SM encourages the Scrum team to improve their development processes and practices within the Scrum process framework in order to be more effective and satisfying in the upcoming sprint. In each sprint retrospective, the Scrum team works out ways to improve product quality by adjusting the DoD accordingly.

At the end of the retrospective, the Scrum team should have worked out improvements for the upcoming sprint. The implementation of these improvements in the next sprint is the adjustment effort for the Scrum team's self-review. Although improvements can be introduced at any time, the retrospective provides a formal framework to focus exclusively on review and adaptation.

4.5.2.7 *Product Backlog Refinement*

PB Refinement — often called grooming — is an ongoing process in which the PO and the Dev Team work together to refine the PB. This includes:

- Ordering entries (PO: by priority, team: by technical dependencies)

- Deleting entries that are no longer important/ necessary

- Adding new entries (can also be architecture-driven)

- Detailing of entries ($\rightarrow$ Definition of Ready, DoR)

- Merging of entries (merge)

- Estimation of entries (Planning Poker)

- Planning of releases

In addition to the PO and the Dev Team, specialists and stakeholders can also be invited to a refinement, for example to explain certain new functionalities to the team.

The Scrum team decides when and how this refinement will take place. It should not take more than 10% of the Dev Team's capacity. The PO can have the entries in the PB updated at any time.

Higher ranked/prioritized PB entries are typically clearer and have more detail. More accurate estimates emerge based on greater clarity and detail. PB entries to be brought to "Done" in the upcoming sprint should have reached DoR. If this is the case, the corresponding PB entries are considered "Ready". They are ready to be selected by the Dev Team during sprint planning.

The Dev Team is responsible for all estimates. The PO can influence the Dev Team to help them understand the

Table 4.1 Effort estimates

	XS	S	M	L	XL	
1	2	3	5	8	13	21
	Trivial	Easy	Medium	Difficult	Very difficult	

entries or compromise. The final estimate is always done by those who will also do the work.

4.5.2.8 Effort estimates and Planning Poker

An important point to be able to plan is the duration of the implementation of the individual sub-functions of a product, on the basis of which one can make an estimate regarding delivery date, costs, and personnel requirements.

However, it is hardly possible to predict exactly how long a certain job will take as long as it is done for the first time. If it contains similarities to a job that has been done before, or if it is very simple and low risk, a prediction can be made that is probably close to the time that will ultimately be needed.

Since one cannot make an exact prediction, one must estimate the time required. An estimate is by definition inaccurate. Therefore, approximations with ratio series are often used for estimation. Often T-shirt sizes and the Fibonacci series are used. It is not estimated in number of person-days, but the complexity is determined.

0	1/2	1	2	3
5	8	13	20	40
100	?	∞	☕	

Figure 4.3: Poker deck.

4.5.2.9 *Story estimates*

To estimate the story, each developer on the Dev Team is given a deck of cards. Each card has a Fibonacci number on it, typically from 1 to 40. The more complex a user story is estimated to be, the higher the Fibonacci number. An example of a complete poker set is shown in figure 4.3.

The meaning of the cards is:

0: There is nothing to do, the story is already implemented

2: Standard size, according to which all can follow

½-100: Different estimated sizes

?: I have no idea, I am still missing important information

∞ : The story is too big or cannot be estimated

BREAK: I need a break

It is important that all participants (the Dev Team members) have the same understanding of the sizes. To achieve this, the team needs to calibrate. To do this, it is best to take a job that has already been done, that is very small, with little complexity, and that is well known to all. Once such a work is found, it is defined as a 2: Standard size, story.

To estimate a story, the PO explains the story to the Dev Team until every Dev Team member is ready to estimate.

- For each user story to be estimated, the developer now draws the card with the estimated complexity without the others seeing it.

- Everyone then reveals their card at the same time.

- In case of disagreement, the members with the highest and lowest estimate explain their rationale.

- The estimation is repeated until a consensus is reached

- The round repeats for each story to be estimated.

If there are a large number of user stories, it is useful to agree on a time limit per story, and monitor each with an hourglass or stopwatch. If the time has expired without the story being estimated, this is an indication that the description is not well understood and should be rewritten.

4.5.3 Sprint Cancelling

Only a PO is authorized to terminate a sprint prematurely. He may do this on the advice of the stakeholders, the Dev Team, or the SM.

If several Scrum teams are running in parallel in a project, aborting is not very advisable, as it is more efficient if all teams have the same rhythm. Aborting should be the last resort. It is advisable to consider renegotiating the sprint goal before aborting.

The reason for aborting is when the sprint goal becomes obsolete. This can be caused, for example, if stakeholders or the company change direction, or if other market or technological conditions change. A sprint should only be aborted if continuation no longer makes sense under the current circumstances. However, given the short duration of sprints, termination rarely makes sense.

If a sprint is aborted, all "Done" PB entries from the sprint backlog are assessed. If some of the work is potentially deliverable, it is usually accepted by the PO. Any incomplete entries go back into the PB and are re-estimated the next time they are included in a sprint backlog. This will include the part of the work that has been done so far and is still usable.

4.6 Scrum Artifacts

Scrum artifacts represent work or business value. They are designed to maximize transparency of key information.

This way, anyone inspecting them has the same basis for alignment. Each artifact is created to provide information that increases transparency and focus against which progress can be measured:

■ For the PB, it's the product goal.

■ For the sprint backlog, it is the sprint goal.

■ For the increment, it's the DoD.

These commitments exist to reinforce empiricism and Scrum values for the Scrum team and its stakeholders.

4.6.1 *Product Backlog*

The PB is an ordered list of everything that can be included in the product. It serves as the single source of requirements for all changes to the product. The PO is responsible for the PB, its contents, access to it, and the order of entries. A PB is never complete. During its initial development steps, it shows only the requirements that are initially known and best understood. The PB evolves with the product and its use. It is dynamic; it continually adapts to ensure that the product is up to its task in order to compete and provide the required benefits. The PB lives as long as the associated product. The PB lists all features, functionalities, enhancements, and bug fixes that make up the changes to the product in future releases. A PB entry contains a description, order, estimate, and value as attributes.

Requirements never stop changing. Therefore, the PB is a living artifact. Changes in requirements from the market can result in changes to the PB.

If multiple Scrum teams are working on a product, a single PB is still used to describe the upcoming work on the product. In this case, it is recommended to use a grouping attribute for the PB entries.

4.6.2 Commitment: Product Goal

The product goal describes a future state of the product that can be used by the Scrum team as a target and for planning. The product goal is located in the PB. The rest of the PB is created to define "what" will fulfill the product goal.

A product is a vehicle to deliver value. It has a clear boundary, known stakeholders, clearly defined users or customers. A product can be a service, a physical product, or something more abstract.

The product goal is the long-term goal for the Scrum team. They must complete (or abandon) one goal before tackling the next.

4.6.2.1 Definition of Ready (DoR)

Each entry should reach DoR status before being scheduled into a sprint. The DoR is an agreement within the Scrum team to indicate that a PB entry is mature enough and all necessary details are included. This can include:

■ An understandable text for the requirement/functionality

- All terminology unambiguously according to known glossary

- Effort estimate provided by the Dev Team (story points)

- Acceptance criteria defined and achievable

- Underlying requirements linked

- Responsibility for acceptance defined

- All known and relevant prerequisites and dependencies noted

4.6.3 Sprint Backlog

The sprint backlog is the set of PB items selected for the sprint, supplemented with the plan for delivering the product increment as well as meeting the sprint goal. The sprint backlog is a forecast by the Dev Team of what functionality will be included in the next increment and the work required to deliver that functionality in a completed increment.

The sprint backlog makes visible all the work that the Dev Team believes is necessary to achieve the sprint goal.

The sprint backlog is a sufficiently detailed plan to be able to see progress within the sprint in the Daily Scrum. The Dev Team adjusts the sprint backlog during the sprint; thus, the sprint backlog evolves during the sprint. This evolution occurs as the Dev Team works through the plan and learns more about the steps still needed to achieve the sprint goal.

As more work is needed, the Dev Team adds it to the sprint backlog. When work is performed or completed, the estimate of remaining work is updated. If components of the plan are found to be unnecessary, they are removed. Only the Dev Team can change its sprint backlog during the sprint. The sprint backlog is a highly visible, real-time picture of the Dev Team's work. It belongs solely to the Dev Team.

4.6.4 Commitment: Sprint Goal

The sprint goal is the single target for the sprint. Although the sprint goal is a commitment for the developers, it provides flexibility in terms of the exact work required to achieve the goal. The sprint goal creates coherence and focus and encourages the Scrum team to work together rather than on separate initiatives.

The sprint goal is created during the sprint planning Event and then added to the sprint backlog. As developers work during the sprint, they keep the sprint goal in mind. If the work turns out to be different than they expected, they work with the PO to adjust the scope of the sprint backlog within the sprint without affecting the sprint goal.

4.6.5 Increment

The increment is the result of all PB entries completed in a sprint and the result of the increments of all previous sprints. At the end of a sprint, the new increment must be "Done"; that is, it must be in a usable state and meet the team's DoD. It must be in a usable state regardless of whether the PO actually wants to deliver it or not. Each increment is additive to all previous increments and thoroughly tested to ensure that all increments work together.

4.6.6 Definition of Done (DoD)

The DoD is a common understanding of the Scrum team under which conditions a work can be considered done. It can vary significantly from Scrum team to Scrum team. Team members on a Scrum team must have a common understanding of when work is considered complete. This ensures transparency. This is also ultimately used to determine when a product increment is complete. The DoD also guides the Dev Team in deciding how many PB entries it can accept during sprint planning. The purpose of each sprint is to deliver increments of potentially shippable functionality that meet the Scrum team's current DoD.

The DoD is established at the beginning of a project and typically includes acceptance/quality criteria, constraints, and general non-functional requirements. As the Scrum team gains experience, the DoD evolves to include more stringent criteria for higher quality. This may include:

- ■ Unit and integration tests
- ■ Architecture documents (design)
- ■ Documentation
- ■ User Guide

Not all DoD criteria have to apply to every user story. During sprint planning, criteria can also be selected individually for each user story, based on which fulfillment it is then decided whether a PB entry can be considered as completed or not.

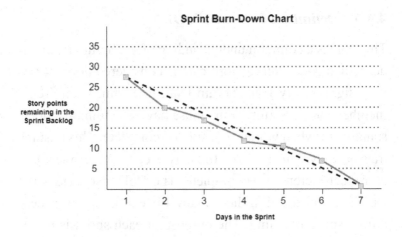

Figure 4.4: Sprint Burn-down chart.

4.7 Progress Control

4.7.1 *Sprint Burn-Down Chart*

The main tool for progress monitoring is the burn-down chart. The burn-down chart is used to visualize work that has already been done and work that remains to be done. The burn-down chart is a chart that compares the completed items per day against the planned completion rate. Its main value is to ensure that the sprint is going according to plan. This technique helps identify issues as they arise. This way, they can be discussed during the daily stand-ups and you can focus on solving them early to keep up with the pace.

Figure 4.4 shows that the Dev Team was unable to complete the planned tasks on the fifth and sixth days, but was back on track on the seventh and eighth days.

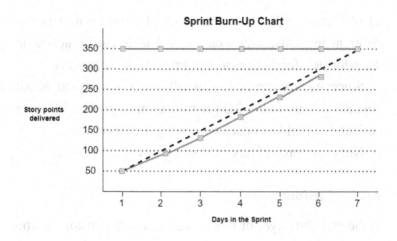

Figure 4.5: Sprint Burn-up chart

4.7.2   Release Burn-Up Chart

Similar to the sprint burn-down chart, a Release Burn-up chart helps estimate how many sprints are needed to complete a project on time and whether the team needs to adjust the estimated time frame. The x axis shows the sprints, while the y axis describes how many stories need to be completed before the final release. Release burn-up is very important when the original PB has been updated with new stories during development. These updates inevitably affect the release date. The chart in figure 4.5 shows that by sprint five, the planned tasks could not be completed, but by day six, the Dev Team was back on schedule.

4.8   Other Stakeholders

From the Scrum team's point of view, all stakeholders can actually be regarded as customers. Work is to be done for all of them equally. However, each of these customers has different interests, which can have a different influence on the priorities depending on the progress of the project.

Since each customer is usually only concerned about himself, it is up to the PO (or project management in larger projects) to build a consensus among the customers.

Not every project has the same types of customers.

4.8.1 Customer

In the end, the buyer or money supplier is the customer who gets the highest priority. In case of priority conflicts, he has to be informed about possible consequences/ impacts. Based on facts that are as complete as possible, he has to decide what he wants to live with.

The product is made available to the customer(s) after completion. Depending on the situation, customers can be internal departments as well as external persons or groups. It is the PO's task to inspire his customers by delivering the desired product. Therefore, the PO and customer should be in close communication for the duration of the project. Before development begins, the PO should gain as accurate an understanding as possible of what his customers want. After the first sprints, customers should already have the opportunity to look at the new functionalities and provide feedback on them.

4.8.2 End User

End users are those persons who use the product. A user can, but does not have to, be a customer at the same time. The role of the user is of particular importance for the Scrum team because only the user can evaluate the product from the user's perspective. Users and customers should be brought in during the sprint review to test the product and provide feedback. They can also be invited to the PB Refinement in order to be able to explain functionalities first-hand or, in the case of high complexity, to be able to provide answers to open questions directly.

4.8.3 Management

Management must not only be a spectator. It must commit to Scrum. It is responsible for ensuring that the framework conditions are right. In addition to providing premises and work equipment, this generally includes supporting the course taken. The management is responsible to protect the Scrum team from external work requirements, to find adequate staffing, as well as to support the SM in clearing obstacles out of the way.

4.8.4 Testing

Testing is a special customer: It has the task of finding as many errors in the product as possible before it goes to the end customer. The aim is to create an environment for close and constructive collaboration between the Scrum team and Testing. This is the basis for a lively exchange. The higher the understanding of testing is, how a requirement was technically implemented by the Dev Team, the more targeted testing can try to break this implementation. However, this technical understanding should be limited to procedures and strategies, and by no means be based on code.

4.9 Limits of Scrum

One criticism of Scrum is that it often does not focus on the quality of the code.

Teams whose members are geographically dispersed or work part-time are less suited to using Scrum. In Scrum, developers should have close and continuous interaction and ideally work together in the same room most of the time. Although recent improvements in technology have reduced the impact of these barriers (for example, the ability to collaborate on a digital whiteboard), the agile manifesto asserts that the best communication is face-to-face.

Teams whose members have very specialized skills are not always suitable for implementation with Scrum. In Scrum, developers should have T-shaped skills that allow them to work on tasks outside their specialization. This can be fostered by good Scrum leadership. While team members with very specific skills can and do contribute well, they should be encouraged to learn more about and collaborate with other disciplines.

Scrum requires breaking product development into short sprints and careful planning; external dependencies, such as user acceptance testing or coordination with other teams, can cause delays and the failure of individual sprints. Products with many external dependencies are therefore less suitable for implementation with Scrum.

Scrum is also less suitable for products that are mature, legacy systems or systems with regulated quality control. In Scrum, product increments should be able to be fully developed and tested in a single sprint; products that require large amounts of regression testing or safety testing with each release (for example, medical devices or vehicle controls) are less suitable for short sprints than for longer waterfall releases.

Chapter 5

Best Practices for the Dev Team

5.1 Version Control

Version control systems (VCs), also called source control or revision control, are software management systems that manage changes in source code, documents, configurations, or other data. Depending on the tool used, the functions vary, but the following functions are available in most of them:

- A complete, long-term history of all changes, which were made to a file.

- Branching and merging: branching or forking allows a branch to be created at a given point in time so that two copies exist and developers can work in different copies. Merging allows changes in one branch to be merged into another.

■ Traceability allows to track any change made to the software and by whom.

■ Check-out/Check-in: Depending on the VCs used, check-out creates a local copy of a file. A developer can choose a specific version to work on. With check-in or commit the local changes are uploaded back into the repository or merged. The VCs will automatically create a new version of the file.

■ Diff allows to highlight the differences in different versions of files or branches.

■ Release creates a "frozen" state so that all files get a specific release version to publish.

Depending on the versioning tool used, other functions are included such as reporting or statistics on changes. It is a best practice that every code which is checked in is compilable and executable.

Today, the use of VCs is essential in each larger software project. They are integrated into the development cycle. For example, nightly build and smoke tests automatically check out, compile, and test the source code.

5.1.1 Branching

Essentially, there are two main reasons to create a branch from the master:

■ **Feature branch:** If new features are disruptive that the whole Dev Team should not be affected by, new features can be developed first in a branch before being merged back into the master.

■ **Fixes branch:** While most development takes place in the master, a fixes branch can be created to fix bugs in an older version of a release.

Most development takes place in the main branch, master or main trunk, depending on the VCS. There should be no branch per developer. As a rule of thumb, you should only create a branch if it is not possible to continue development in a branch.

The Git documentation says exactly the opposite. For small changes or bug fixes, too you should create a local branch. This requires that the developers have agreed on who is working on which code or feature to avoid merge conflicts and duplicates.

5.1.2 Git

Git is a distributed VCs and is the most widely used VCs today. Git has a higher learning curve than other VCSs, but it makes branching and merging much easier. It also does not create a complete copy of the master. To switch between two branches with Git, the developer doesn't have to change directories but just issue the Git switch command to switch to the branch they want to work with.

Git can be used both from the command line and from a graphical user interface. There are online versions of Git, GitHub and GitLab. GitHub and GitLab are both popular, web-based Git repositories that offer Continuous Integration and Continuous Delivery (CI/CD).

5.1.3 Subversion

Subversion or SVN is a central VCS. SVN is reliable and secure and is also used by a large number of developers. It is the most commonly used centralized VCS. It is considered the simplest VCS, but its branch management consumes a lot of resources on the central server. It is a little slower than distributed VCS.

5.2 Software Quality

Software quality refers to two related areas:

■ **Functional quality** refers to how well it meets or conforms to a given design, based on functional requirements or specifications. This refers to the usability of the software.

■ The **structural quality** of software refers to how well it meets non-functional requirements that support the fulfillment of functional requirements, such as stability or maintainability.

Software quality plays an important role especially when a software reaches a certain size and complexity. Important characteristics of the software quality are:

■ **Stability:** How often do new bugs occur

■ **Maintainability:** How readable/understandable is the code

Figure 5.1: ISO software quality model

- ■ **Extensibility:** How well new functions can be programmed in addition

In order to ensure a high measure of software quality, software quality models were formed. A well-known model was developed by the ISO and is represented in illustration figure 5.1.

A given software quality model is often helpful for gaining a holistic understanding of software quality. In practice, the relative importance of certain software properties typically depends on the software domain, the product type, and the intended use. Therefore, software properties should be defined for each product and used as a guide for development. To keep software quality high, best practices have been established, informal rules which have proven themselves in practice.

5.2.1 Coding Guidelines

Better code readability over the entire project is achieved by allowing the eye to get used to one style of the code.

For this purpose, company/project-wide guidelines should be defined as to what form the code should take. These coding standards/guidelines should be created per language and should be formulated in a way that is easy to read and understand. The number of rules should be limited so that they can be remembered: 30 — 50 rules have proven to be an upper limit.

5.2.2 KISS

A very simple way to keep maintainability high is to always keep the Keep it simple and stupid (KISS) principle in mind. That is, you should always ask yourself if there is a simpler way to implement a specific problem. Simple solutions reduce complexity, increase stability, improve readability of the code, and diminish the workload of the developers, especially the ones working on existing code.

5.2.3 Clean Code

Clean code is a paradigm in software engineering originating in the book with the same name by Robert Martin [6]. It describes principles, patterns, and practices of writing clean code.

Clean code means:

■ Low cyclomatic complexity

Cyclomatic complexity is a software metric used to indicate the complexity of a program. It is a quantitative measure of the number of linearly independent paths through a program's source code.

■ Readable code (meaningful names)

Only meaningful names should be used. The name of a variable, a function or a class should answer all important questions. It should say why a class or function exists, what it does, and how it is used. If a name requires a comment, then the name does not reveal its intent.

■ Maintainable code

Maintainability refers to the ease with which software code can be repaired, improved, and understood.

■ Testable code

Testability refers to the ease with which code can be tested. Smaller functions are usually easier to test than complex ones. If a unit test requires a lot of initialization effort before the test can be executed, then this is a sign that the code is too complex.

5.3   SOLID Principles

The SOLID principles are five design principles that are intended to make object-oriented software designs more understandable, flexible, and maintainable.

The five principles are a subset of principles published by software engineer Robert C. Martin.

5.3.1 Single Responsibility Principle

The single responsibility principle states that each class should have only one responsibility.

More than one responsibility for a class leads to multiple areas where future changes may be necessary. The likelihood that the class will need to be changed at a later date increases along with the risk of introducing subtle errors when making such changes. This principle usually leads to classes with high cohesion, in which all methods have a strong common reference.

5.3.2 Open-Closed Principle

The open-closed principle states that software entities such as modules, classes, and methods, should allow extensions (be open to them), but without changing their behavior, that is their source code and interface should not change. The open-closed principle was formulated in 1988 by Bertrand Meyer.

An extension in the sense of the open-closed principle is for example inheritance. This does not change the existing behavior of a class, but extends it with additional functions or data. Overwritten methods do not change the behavior of the basis class, but only that of the derived class. Going one step further, according to the Liskov substitution principle (LSP), overwritten methods too do not change the behavior, but only the algorithms.

5.3.3 Liskov Substitution Principle

The LSP, or substitutability principle, requires that an instance of a derived class behaves in such a way that someone who thinks they have an object of the base class in front of them is not surprised by unexpected behavior when it is actually an object of a subtype. It was formulated in 1993 by Barbara Liskov and Jeannette Wing.

Object-oriented programming languages cannot a priori rule out a violation of this principle, which can occur because of the polymorphism associated with inheritance. Often a violation of the principle is not obvious at first sight.

5.3.4 Interface Segregation Principle

The interface segregation principle is used to split up interfaces that are too large. The segregation should be done according to the clients' requirements for the interfaces and in such a way that the new interfaces fit exactly to the requirements of the individual clients. So, the clients only have to deal with interfaces that can do what, and only what, the clients need. The principle was formulated by Robert C. Martin in 1996. With the help of the interface segregation principle it, is possible to divide a software in such a way into decoupled and thus more easily refactorable classes that future functional or technical requirements to the software need only small changes to the software.

5.3.5 Dependency Inversion Principle

The dependency inversion principle deals with the reduction of coupling of modules. It states that dependencies should always be directed from more concrete modules of lower levels to abstract modules of higher levels.

This ensures that dependency relationships always run in one direction, from concrete to abstract modules and from derived classes to base classes. This reduces dependencies between modules and avoids cyclic dependencies in particular.

5.4 Design Patterns

A design pattern is a generalized, reusable solution to a common problem within a particular context in software design. It is not a finished design that can be converted directly into source or machine code. Rather, it is a description or template for solving a problem that can be used in many different situations. Design patterns are formalized best practices that programmers can use to solve common problems when designing an application or system.

Object-oriented design patterns typically show relationships and interactions between classes or objects without specifying the final application classes or objects involved. Patterns that imply mutable state may be inappropriate for functional programming languages, some patterns may be redundant in languages that have built-in support for solving the problem they are trying to solve, and object-oriented patterns may not be appropriate for non-object-oriented languages.

Design patterns fall into three categories, depending on the problem they solve: creational patterns, structural patterns, and behavioral patterns. There are others such as concurrency patterns, but they might be considered behavioral patterns too.

5.4.1 Creational Patterns

Creational design patterns are design patterns that deal with the creation of an object and attempt to create objects in a way that is appropriate to the situation. The basic form of object creation could lead to design problems or additional design complexity. Creational design patterns solve this problem by controlling this object generation.

Creational patterns are composed of two dominant ideas. One is encapsulating the knowledge of what concrete classes the system uses. Another is hiding how instances of these concrete classes are created and combined.

Examples of creational patterns are:

■ Abstract Factory
  Creates an instance of different families of classes

■ Builder
  Separates the object instantiation from its representation

■ Factory Method
  Creates an instance of various derived classes

■ Object Pool
   Avoids the acquisition and release of resources by re-cycling objects that are no longer needed

■ Prototype
   Copies or clones a fully instantiated object

■ Singleton
   A class of which there may be only one instance.

5.4.2 *Structural Patterns*

Structural patterns are design patterns that facilitate design by providing a simple way to realize relationships between entities. Examples of structural patterns are:

■ Adapter
   Adapt interfaces of different classes

■ Bridge
   Separates the interface of an object from its imple-mentation

■ Composite
   A tree structure of simple and composite objects

■ Decorator
   Dynamically add responsibilities to an object

■ Facade
   A class representing an entire subsystem

■ Flyweight
   A fine-grained instance for efficient sharing

■ Private Class Data
Restricts the access of accessors/mutators

■ Proxy
An object that represents another object

5.4.3 Behavioral Patterns

Behavioral design patterns are design patterns that identify common communication patterns between objects. As a result, these patterns increase flexibility in how communication is performed.

Examples of behavioral patterns are:

■ Chain of responsibility
A way to pass a request between a chain of objects.

■ Command
Encapsulates a command request as an object

■ Interpreter
Defines a grammatical representation of a language and an interpreter to interpret the grammar

■ Iterator
Sequentially accesses the elements of a collection

■ Mediator
Defines a simplified communication between classes

■ Memento
Capture and restore the internal state of an object

■ Null Object
Represents the default value of an object

■ Observer

Communicate a change to a number of classes

■ State

Change the behavior of an object when the state changes

■ Strategy

Encapsulates an algorithm in a class

■ Template Method

Move the exact steps of an algorithm into a subclass

■ Visitor

Define a new operation without changing the class

5.4.4 Concurrency Patterns

Concurrency patterns are design patterns that deal with multithreaded programming.

Examples of concurrency patterns are:

■ Actor Model

Actors communicate with messages, not shared memory

■ Event Loop

Blocks on the event provider and sends an event to an event handler on arrival

Design patterns are well documented, and many implementation samples can be found on the Internet.

5.5   Continuous Integration/Continuous Delivery

Continuous Integration/Continuous Delivery or Deployment (CI/CD) refers to a culture, set of operating principles, and collection of practices that enable application development teams to deliver code changes more frequently and reliably. Deployment is also known as the CI/CD pipeline. CI/CD has become a quasi standard in software development today.

CI/CD connects the activities of the development and operations teams through automation in building, testing, and deploying applications. Modern DevOps practices, see section 5.6, include continuous development, continuous testing, CI, CD, and continuous monitoring of software applications throughout their development lifecycle. The CI/CD practice or CI/CD pipeline forms the backbone of modern DevOps operations.

CI/CD is also a best practice of agile methodology as it allows software development teams to focus on meeting business requirements, code quality, and security as deployment steps are automated.

CI is a coding philosophy and set of practices that drive development teams to implement small changes and check in code frequently to version control repositories. Since most modern applications require code to be developed across multiple platforms and tools, the team needs a mechanism to integrate and validate their changes.

The technical goal of CI is to establish a consistent and automated method for building, packaging, and testing applications. When a consistent integration process is in place, teams are more likely to commit code changes more frequently, leading to better collaboration and software quality.

CD picks up where CI leaves off. CD automates the delivery of applications to selected infrastructure environments. Most teams work with multiple environments besides the production environment, such as development and test environments, and CD ensures there is an automated way to push code changes to these environments.

CI/CD tools help store the environment-specific parameters that need to be packaged with each delivery. CI/CD automation then makes any necessary service calls to web servers, databases, and other services that may need to be restarted or follow different procedures as applications are deployed.

CI/CD require continuous testing because the goal is to deliver high-quality applications and code to users. Continuous testing is often implemented as a series of automated regression, performance, and other tests that are run in the CI/CD pipeline, see Chapter 6.

5.6 DevOps

DevOps is a combination of practices from software development and information technology (IT) operations. DevOps is a portmanteau word composed of development and operations. DevOps is the combination of cultural philosophies, practices, and tools that increases an organization's ability to deliver applications and services at high speed: Products are developed and improved faster than companies using traditional software development and infrastructure management processes. This speed enables companies to better serve their customers and compete more effectively in the marketplace.

In a DevOps model, development and operations teams are no longer "siloed". Sometimes these two teams are merged into a single team where engineers work across the entire application lifecycle, from development and testing to deployment and operations, developing a set of skills that are not limited to a single function.

In some DevOps models, quality assurance and security teams can also be more closely integrated into development and operations as well as the entire application lifecycle. When security is the focus of all members of a DevOps team, it is sometimes referred to as DevSecOps. These teams use practices to automate processes that were manual and slow in the past. They use a technology stack and tools that help them run and evolve applications quickly and reliably. These tools also help engineers complete tasks on their own (such as deploying code or provisioning infrastructure) that would have normally required help from other teams, further increasing a team's speed.

5.7 Security Checkers

Source code analysis tools, also called static application security testing (SAST) tools, are used to analyze source code or compiled versions of code to find security vulnerabilities.

Some tools are already included in the Integrated Development Environment (IDE). For security issues that can be detected during the software development phase itself, this is a powerful way to detect security vulnerabilities within the development lifecycle because they provide immediate feedback to the developer about issues they may introduce into the code during development. This immediate feedback is very helpful as vulnerabilities are found later in the development lifecycle.

Another option is to include a source code analysis tool in the nightly build and smoke tests. This way the developers automatically get feedback about possible vulnerabilities in the code.

There are a variety of analysis tools. On the Open Web Application Security Project (OWASP) website, you can find a list of tools, some are free open source and others are commercial. Modern security analysis tools use machine learning techniques for finding possible weaknesses and vulnerabilities.

Advantages of SAST tools include:

■ In general, they scale well — they can be applied to a large amount of software and run repeatedly, for example as part of CI.

■ They find vulnerabilities such as buffer overflows, Structured Query Language (SQL) injection flaws or cross-site scripting (XSS).

■ The output shows developers exactly where in the source code the problem exists.

Disadvantages are:

■ Many security vulnerabilities are difficult to find automatically, for example authentication problems, access control issues, and insecure use of cryptography. With the current state of the art, such tools can only find a relatively small percentage of application security vulnerabilities automatically. However, tools of this type are getting better and better.

■ High number of false positives.

■ Often configuration issues cannot be found because they are not in the code.

■ Many of these tools have difficulty analyzing code that cannot be compiled. Analysts often can't compile code because they don't have the right libraries, all the compilation instructions, all the source code, etc.

Security checkers do not replace run-time security monitoring tools, and Web Application Firewalls (WAF), Log File Analyzer, or Intrusion Detection Systems (IDS) are still a necessity.

Chapter 6

Testing

Depending on the literature, there are at least three levels of testing: Unit testing, integration testing, and system testing. Often a fourth level, acceptance testing is included by developers. This may take the form of operational acceptance testing or simple end user (beta) testing to ensure that the software meets functional expectations. Tests are often assigned to one of these levels based on where in the software development process they are added or the level of specificity of the test.

Traditional and agile testing can be compared with the test pyramid in figure 6.1. In traditional software testing, the vast majority of testing is done using test plans to manually test the system through the user interface. In the middle

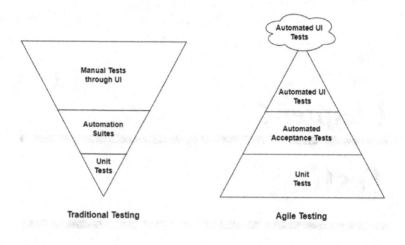

Figure 6.1: Test pyramid.

layer, there may be some automated tests using test suites. There may also be some unit testing by developers.

Unlike in waterfall methods, in agile software development, testing can start at the beginning of the project with Continuous Integration between development and testing. Agile testing is not only sequential but also continuous. Agile testing is focused on avoiding bugs, whereas traditional testing is focused on finding bugs.

6.1 Unit Testing

Unit testing verifies the functionality of a particular section of code, usually at the function level. In an object-oriented environment, this is usually at the class level, and the minimum unit tests include the constructors and destructors. In agile testing, the goal is to have full test coverage of all public and protected methods or functions.

Unit tests are usually written by developers as they work on the code (white-box tests) to ensure that the specific function works as expected. A function may have multiple tests to catch corner cases or other branching in the code. Unit tests alone cannot verify the functionality of a piece of software, but are used to ensure that the building blocks of the software work independently of each other.

6.2   Integration Testing

In integration testing, software modules are logically integrated and tested as a group. A typical software project consists of several software modules developed by different programmers. The purpose of integration testing is to detect errors in the interaction between these software modules as they are integrated.

Integration testing focuses on checking the data communication between these modules. Therefore, integration testing is also referred to as "I & T" (Integration and Testing), "String Testing", or "Thread Testing".

6.3   System Testing

System testing is a type of black-box testing in which the complete and fully integrated software product is tested. The purpose of system testing is to validate the end-to-end system specifications. Usually, the software is only one element of a larger computer-based system. The software is connected to other software/hardware systems. System testing is a series of different tests whose purpose is to test the entire computer-based system.

6.4 User Acceptance Testing (UAT)

UAT is a type of testing that is performed by end users or by the customer to verify/accept the software system before the software application is transferred to the production environment. UAT is performed in the final phase of testing after functional, integration, and system testing, are complete. UATs are often performed in the customer environment.

The main purpose of UAT is to validate end-to-end business processes. UAT does not focus on cosmetic bugs, spelling errors, or system testing. UAT is performed in a separate test environment with production-like data setup (pre-production). It is a type of black-box testing involving two or more end users.

6.5 Regression Testing

Regression testing verifies that a recent program or code change has no negative impact on existing functionality. Regression testing is a complete or partial selection of previously executed test cases that are re-executed to ensure that existing functionality works properly, for example, after reengineering.

These tests are performed to ensure that new code changes have no side effects on existing functionality. It is ensured that the old code still works after code changes have been made.

6.6 Exploratory Testing

In exploratory testing, the test cases are not created in advance, but the testers of the system perform the tests "on the fly". The testers may jot down ideas about what to test before testing. Sometimes brainstorming takes place before testing. The focus of exploratory testing is more on testing as a "thinking" activity (brain activity).

Exploratory testing is widely used in agile methodologies and revolves around discovery, investigation, and learning. It emphasizes the personal freedom and responsibility of the individual tester.

In scripted testing, test engineers first design test cases, which are executed during testing. In contrast, in exploratory testing, test design and test execution are performed simultaneously.

Scripted test execution is usually a non-thinking activity in which testers execute the test steps and compare the actual results with the expected results. Such test execution activity can be automated and does not require many cognitive skills.

Exploratory testing is manual testing that relies on the tester's experience.

There are many more types of tests. In agile testing, there are a variety of other types of tests which are beyond the scope of this script.

Appendix A

Appendix

A.1   Scrum Terms

Here are the most important Scrum terms listed again:

A.1.1   Scrum Team

- **Product Owner (PO):** Interfaces with customers, and manages requirements and their prioritization

- **Development Team (Dev Team):** Implements the requirements

- **Scrum Master (SM):** Responsible for the correct implementation of Scrum and empowers the Scrum team

A.1.2   Scrum Events

- **Time Box:** Specified maximum duration for a Scrum event, which should not be exceeded.

DOI: 10.1201/9781003301707-A

- **Sprint:** Cycle in which a finished product increment is produced. Includes all other Scrum events. Fixed time box.

- **Sprint Planning:** Overall planning for the current Sprint. Time box varies depending on Sprint length.

- **Daily Scrum (Stand-up):** Synchronization meeting in stand-up for the Dev Team. Fixed time box of 15 minutes.

- **Sprint Review (Sprint Demo):** Presentation of the product increment, working out the next steps. Time box varies depending on sprint length.

- **Sprint Retrospective:** Review of the past Sprint for the Scrum team to work out improvements for the future. Time box varies depending on the sprint length.

- **Planning Poker:** Dynamic method for estimating effort.

A.1.3 Scrum Artifacts

- **Product Backlog (PB):** Prioritized list of requirements, the PB entries.

- **Sprint Backlog:** An excerpt from the PB that is to be completed in the new Sprint.

- **PB item (PBI):** An entry in the PB that describes a requirement. The scope and complexity are selected so that the PBI can be completed within a Sprint.

■ **Product increment:** The sum of all PBIs completed in the Sprint with the product increments of all previous Sprints at the end of the current Sprint.

■ **Burn-Down Charts:** Visualization of the work status.

■ **Epic:** Summarizing related use cases.

■ **Story Points:** Unit of effort estimates for the Dev Team.

A.1.4 Other Terms

■ **Definition of Ready (DoR):** State of a PBI. Defined by the Scrum team and further refined over the duration of the project. Defines a state that a PBI must have before it can be included in the Sprint Backlog.

■ **Definition of Done (DoD):** State of a PBI. Defined by the Scrum team and further refined over the duration of the project. Defines a state that the implementation of a PBI must have in order for the PBI to be considered completed or "Done".

■ **Scrum Board:** Overview of current tasks.

■ **Use Cases:** Describe use cases, and requirements from customer/user perspective.

A.2 Comparison of Classical vs. Agile Methods

In summary, the most important differences of agile vs. classic methods are listed in table A.1.

Table A.1   Classical vs. agile methods

Classical	Agile
Requirements known at the beginning	Requirements fuzzy at the beginning
Changes to requirements during the course of the project difficult (change request)	Changes to requirements during the course of the project scheduled
Often high costs for late requirement changes	Mostly moderate costs for late requirement changes
Requirements description from technical point of view (features)	Requirements description from customer/user point of view (user stories)
Sequential development process	Iterative development process
Rigid project management process	Continuous process improvements
Customer sees only end result	Customer evaluates intermediate results
If it gets tight, rather push milestones	If it gets tight, rather reduce effort
Large teams possible	Relatively small teams necessary
Clear hierarchy	Self-organized teams
Many specialists in the team	Much shared responsibility

(*Continued on next page*)

Table A.1 (Continued)

Classical	Agile
Team is distributed and active in several projects	Team sits together and focuses on one project
Assign tasks from above	Take over tasks independently
Much communication via documents and long meetings	Much informal communication and stand-up meetings
Effort estimation by project manager or experts	Effort estimation together in team

References

[1] Schwaber, K & Sutherland, J 2020, The Scrum Guide.

[2] The Agile Manifesto, 2001–2021, https://www.agilealliance.org/agile101/the-agile-manifesto/>.

[3] 12 Principles Behind the Agile Manifesto, https://www.agilealliance.org/agile101/12-principles-behind-the-agile-manifesto/>.

[4] Agile Alliance, 2001, https://www.agilealliance.org>.

[5] 'Extreme Programming: A gentle introduction', 2013.

[6] Martin, R 2019, Clean Code, Pearson Education.

Index

Printed in the United States
by Baker & Taylor Publisher Services